AUSTRALIAN ENTREPRENEUR

Zackeri Leitmann

To the people who supported me - Thank you.
To the people who didn't - Fuck you.
To everyone else - Watch this.

PREFACE

In this document, I'm going to attempt to spare you unnecessary jargon and wordy bullshit. That's just not how I operate. I'm just trying to convey my process and help you along your journey. So, what I'm going to dois explain it simply and coherently for the average person. It doesn't matter if you've just left high school or you decided your boss for the last 10 years can stick it up their ass because you can do a better job.

This is the new business field guide. Follow along as we proceed, you will need to cross-reference multiple steps a few times. It may seem daunting at first, but I guarantee you won't regret it.

"If you can't explain it simply, you don't understand it well enough." ~ Einstein

ABOUT ME:

As much as I don't like the term "entrepreneur" because in modern society it's used out of context; I'm just that, an entrepreneur. The reason I don't like the term is because people use it in the wrong context. It doesn't hold the same value it once did. I'm going to piss a few people off by saying this, but being part of a pyramid scheme/MLM doesn't count. Create something from nothing and earn the title.

I've lived in many countries but was born in Australia. I started my entrepreneurial lifestyle at a very young age mowing lawns and selling avocados from a stall out the front of my house and parents' restaurant. At the time, I was a young child, we weren't rich, my family came from a long line of dairy farmers. That being said, my parents managed to provide my sibling and I with the things we needed and sometimes the things we wanted. I'm very grateful for that, but I wanted to carve my own path. My friends always had the newest toys, the best consoles, and the shiniest bikes. So, I set out to have what they didn't, their own money.

I would mow the lawns of neighbors and the local kindergarten and primary school. I also fabricated a makeshift stall and sold avocados from a tree we had in our back yard. I ran this stall early mornings, weekends, and even set up shop out the front of my parents' restaurant and sold to people passing by on the street.

Before I knew it, I was the only kid my age with over $100 in his pocket at almost any given point. This doesn't seem like much as an adult, but at 11/12 years old, that was insane.

I always had a different lease on life, I've always disliked authority and as a child vowed to never be an employee in the long term,

I wanted to be the boss.

This has been apparent throughout my entire life, I always hated school, because I saw no point in the traditional narrative; get good grades, go to university, get a good job, get a wife, a house, a family, save money, retire.

I've always questioned the status quo, as a child, teachers would label me as someone who "disrupts the class but has amazing potential if he could just focus on the task at hand".

I was focused, but I had already finished the set-out work as it was being written on the board, then for the rest of the lesson, I would be contemplating the world, society, popular culture, etc.

Skip forward.

I left school, worked, did some courses.

Then decided the workforce wasn't for me, so I returned to school and finished high school. I graduated with a good grades. I then set off for university and hated it, I loved the people I met along the way but once again, the narrative wasn't for me.

I dropped out of university after sustaining a serious leg injry. At this point, you must be thinking "Jesus Christ, what's wrong with you?" My parents were not impressed, but I had other plans. I took a part-time gig as a pizza delivery driver "oh, how the mighty have fallen."

During this time, my friend and I came up with an idea for a business, I did a short course on business management. I had everything ready to go, money, paperwork, ABN, location, everything. Then out of the blue at the 11th hour, my business partner bailed on me. Shortly after that, my parents separated and all my work went down the drain, I was in debt and wasn't even 20 yet.

I stayed with my mother who is, to this day, my closest friend and the only person other than my partner who has always supported me.

We sold the house and moved somewhere with more work prospects. We both got jobs co-managing a restaurant. It was decent money, a good team, and I learned a lot from the hands-on experience. After a few months, the owner decided to sell the business. Upon handover, the new owner cleared out all the staff except the chef.

Once again, we were stuck. I, however, kept my ear to the ground about potential opportunities.

Before I knew it, I was filling a void in the town. The local school didn't have a tuck-shop (Australian for canteen, or cafeteria).

So, I pooled my knowledge, wrote a business plan, used suppliers from the restaurant I was managing, and sat down with the school board. They loved my pitch, so I started to get the ball rolling. I had no funding behind me, so I held carcasses and sausage sizzle BBQ events in the community until I raised enough capital. The business took off, I was making good money, had very low overheads, and all my staff was parent volunteers. I built the business to the point where it was autonomous. Then I took a side hustle sales gig. My first day on the job, I was the passenger in a car accident. I sustained a serious neck injury, spent over a month in a neck brace and still today this day suffer from chronic pain.

If that wasn't bad enough, my volunteers left the following week and i had to clsoe down my business. Atleast I had some profits left over. My mother and I moved back to our original town.

Once again, tragedy struck. My mother was admitted to hospital and had her leg amputated. During this time, I lost my job working at the local radio station. We lost our rental house, mum was in the hospital and I was homeless, living out of my car with our pets.

Since that time, I've developed a diverse investment portfolio, founded multiple businesses, and currently the Co-founding CEO of a new product startup. I'm also founding a tech startup.

I was going to leave that section about myself out, but I wanted to show you something. No matter what your circumstances are, no matter what life throws at you, if you persist, you will prevail.

Enough about my origin story, let's talk about yours. You might be on the fence about starting a business, I say do it!

Indeed, you may not succeed at first, I sure didn't, but from that failure, I learned how to succeed. Don't let the potential of failure stop you from trying.

In this book, I'm going to outline some strategies I have used and also give you a good starting point and directions for building your first business in Australia.

CHAPTER 1: THE IDEA

This is as far as most people get, and it breaks my heart. On any given day, you might stumble across a million or billion-dollar idea. Then what happens? Will you be the one to bring it to life?

I want you to think to yourself, does it exist, if so, could it be improved? What's the demand? How will you market it?

I'm going to assume you're a revolutionary, like myself. You've got an idea for a new product, app, start-up, service, or something of the like. You've come up with something that will help the world, fill a need, or increase the quality of life for someone or a demographic of people.

Let's get started, I want you to make a digital document, or take a pencil and paper and write down everything about the idea and don't leave out any details. Brainstorm everything, pros, and cons.

Here are a few things to get you started.

What does it do?

Who is it for?

How does it work?

When will it be available/running?

Where will it be available/located?

If it's an invention, will you need intellectual property or a patent?

If it is technology-based, do you have the required software and hardware?

Do you have the skills required to get the job done? Do you know anyone who does have those skills? Can you learn those skills?

Now that you've got the genius juices flowing I'm going to assume you've got an extensive list of pros and cons, and you've hashed out the idea. From this moment on, the idea is liquid. When I say liquid I mean the idea is subject to evolution. Think of it as the prototype, and version 2, 3, 4, or 5 might be the final product. I wish I could count on one hand the majority of the evolutionary steps of my ideas have gone through before they became reality.

Congratulations, you've now made it further than 99% of people who have a good or even great idea. The cogs are turning, you've set off a chain of events that can take you to places you could never imagine. Take a moment to celebrate, I know that may seem counterproductive, but trust me, each step is a victory and you should be proud of your accomplishments. The last thing you want is to burn out taking some time to revel in your achievement will help you to remain focused, and will help rewire your brain in the long term. To win the war, you must win a series of battles, this is one of them.

A word of caution before we proceed.

I know this can be incredibly exciting, and you'll want to scream from the top of the highest building. DO NOT do that! Tell only the people you trust most, don't post it on social media. Anonymity is your greatest ally. I've been at this point more than once and I've told the wrong people in a haze of excitement, next thing I know, someone with more influence, or money has taken my idea or plan from beneath my feet. The last thing you want is for your billion-dollar idea to fall into the hands of someone with more resources. Keep everything you do low-key. If people ask what you're doing, tell them you're working on some extracurricular research. Don't give everything away, don't boast. Show only your hard work, and the results.

Think of everything like a game of chess, never give away your next move, always plan and have contingencies in place if something goes wrong.

CHAPTER 2: THE PLAN

I hope you've taken the time to reflect on your previous achievement because now the real work begins.

This, for some people, is the most daunting part, and its where a lot of people's ideas, passion, and motivation die. If you can make it past this step, you're well on your way towards being a successful entrepreneur.

The business plan.

This document, while being liquid, is what separates the world of fantasy and reality.

The plan serves as the entire foundation, layout, and future direction of your business. It would be wise to update this continuously and refer to it whenever you're unsure about something.

How do I write a business plan? You have a few options:

You can wing it; I recommend against doing this.

There are a variety of free templates online.

Microsoft Word, and most word processing software have templates available.

Alternatively, you can seek the help of a professional. This can be costly but worthwhile.

For someone new to the business world, with limited funds, I would recommend using Microsoft Word. Their business plans have a good layout, they're customizable and provide you with a solid insight into what should be within each section. If you want a solid business plan, I would recommend investing your time into it. These documents aren't something you can just whip together in 20 minutes; they need to be thoroughly thought out. This is where your pros and cons brainstorming will come into play. By cross-referencing the fundamental principles of your idea, you will develop a more structured plan for moving forwards. This will likely also give you more insight into what comes next, and may even alter your original idea into something similar but more viable.

Here's a list of things that should be included in any high quality business plan. I could write an entire book just on these concepts; so I won't elaborate. That being said, you will find explanations to majority of the below mentioned segments in any decent template.

Executive summary:
Business objectives
Mission statement
Guiding principles

Company description:
Ownership
Start-up summary
Location and facilities

Services:
Daily operations and procedures
Competitive comparison
Suppliers
Management controls
Administrative systems
Future services
Marketing strategy and implimentation:
Strengths
Weaknesses
Opportunities
Threats
Strategy pyramid

USP (Unique selling position)
Competitive edge
Pricing strategy
Promoitonal strategy

Financial plan:
Start-up costs
Source and use of funds
Sale forecast
Profit and loss forecast

I could write a book on each of these things, but that's not what it's about. Keep it short, and to the point. There's no need for wordy waffling.

CHAPTER 3:
PAPER HOOPS

The proverbial "paper hoops", are the government regulations you must abide by to develop a legitimate business. Over many years I have spent hours scouring the internet and never found a coherent guide. I'm writing this in the hopes that you'll save time, learn from my experiences, and not resort to pulling out your hair. It's a win-win.

In Australia, we have an ABN (Australian business number) this is absolutely vital, you will use it on nearly all your documents and paperwork from this point forward. This number acts as the I.D for your business for everything.

It is free to apply online via ASIC (Australian Securities and investment commission) website and you'll get confirmation within 48-72 hours. Some services will try to charge you, don't fall for it, they aren't necessary. Pay close attention to the details when filling out this form. For inexperienced people, I would consider applying for a sole trader pty.ltd (proprietary limited) business. Proprietary limited means that if something bad happens and your business fails, you can liquidate all the business assets and you aren't responsible for debt incurred.

This is subject to debt arrangements, and legislative changes. Do your research and don't hesitate to have a lawyer look over anything before you sign.

Do some research on the type of businesses available and pick whatever suits your situation closest.

To fill out the ABN application, you will need your details, including, but not limited to ID, address, TFN (tax file number).

It's a rather simple process, however, some people just aren't good with paperwork and that's okay too. While not recommended, you can have someone else help you, preferably someone you would trust with your life, because that's the information you're entering. Be careful with who you give your details to. A close family member would be the ideal go-to. When filling out the application, refer to your business plan and choose very carefully about what type of business you are going to be running. What category would it fall under? Retail, manufacturing, etc.

I'm going to assume you've completed this step and now have an ABN. From this point, you can choose to register your business name (also via ASIC) register for GST (Goods and services tax), and register for many other tax benefits, also.

Registering a business name will incur a fee

Now that you have an ABN, and your business name is registered, I would highly recommend heading to the ABLIS (Australian business licenses and information service) website and using their guided search to find any licensing your business will need. This will include council requirements and state regulations. These will vary depending on the nature of your business and may vary from state to state, while some may come under countrywide regulations.

Make sure you stay up to date on licensing regulations. Checking once a month should be adequate and will save you from having to backtrack, in the future. This process will also set your business apart from other startups when pitching to potential buyers, investors, or partners because you're already regulation-compliant and will take you to the next level of legitimacy.

Now, let's say that your idea is an invention or innovation. You might have grounds to patent your process, service, or innovation. To find if your idea already exists, I would recommend going to Google patents and typing some keywords into the search regarding your invention or idea. Doing so will allow you to find out whether or not the idea already exists. If it does exist and is the intellectual property of someone or a business entity, don't lose hope. Read through the patent very carefully, and apply your pros and cons brainstorm and business plan you've already created to see if your idea is different. Many times, your idea might be similar but it may have key differences the set it apart from the existing patent/s. Submitting patents can be highly lucrative for dividends in the long term but can put you out of pocket between $10k - $20k. I would highly recommend seeking out legal counsel on this matter. In regards to this, you will want to find an IP (intellectual property) lawyer or legal firm. They will also be the ones responsible for submitting your IP claim.

CHAPTER 4: RESEARCH AND DEVELOPMENT

So, you're regulation-compliant, have all the paperwork sorted and you are ready to bring your idea to life. This is the R&D (research and development) phase.

Once again, we're going to do another brainstorm, this time it will be a little different.

Start with your idea, think about what it will take to manufacture. Are there any local, state, interstate, or international manufacturers, for similar products?

Depending on your idea this may vary drastically.

For example, if you're starting a food-based business, you won't need a manufacturing facility, but you will likely need to source a distribution outlet or wholesaler. You've got a great menu, so be it. What does each item cost to make? (Including time preparation time and cleaning)

Will you need packaging, serviettes, condiments?

Don't leave out any minor details and work everything out to a point of profit.

In the food industry, your overall costs should be 33% or under.

This will give you. solid profit margin to help cover operating costs, licensing, and other overheads.

If you're starting a retail outlet, what stock will you have? Who will your suppliers be? Do you have a niche? What's your target demographic? Do you have a retail outlet location in mind?

If you're going to be an online retailer, have you considered branded drop shipping, and do you have a website?

If you're developing a new product, what materials will you need?

Can you manufacture it by yourself or will you need a facility or factory to do so?

Will you require packaging?

What is your shipping logistics?

Will you have the space to store inventory?

Does your product or service require public input or testing? If so, have you considered physical or online surveys?

These are just some examples of the thought process needed to bring ideas to life. I'm a firm believer of "question everything" and that mindset will be integral in your entrepreneurial development.

CHAPTER 5: GET BRANDED

I'm going to assume you've come up with a somewhat decent name for your business and maybe even a slogan. Now let's start on a logo and full branding materials. Everything your business does and releases to the world should have your brand on it. A brand is like a social identifier for a business, it's how people recognize your company.

I highly recommend using "Canva" or other free photo editing software, if you don't have a full version of photoshop.

Let's start with the logo, you're going to want something that represents your business. An image or icon that can be interpreted into what your business stands for and aims to get across. If you have a food company, don't have a tech-based logo, it's going to be confusing for customers to associate your brand with food.

I highly recommend using complementary colors in your logo.

It would be a good move to research color theory as different colors can fall under a warm or cold category. There have also been studies showing that certain colors can positively affect people's moods.

Here's a list of how some colors can influence mood (Courtesy of 99 Designs.com):

Red makes you feel passionate and energized.

Red is the warmest and most dynamic of the colors—it triggers opposing emotions. It is often associated with passion and love as well as anger and danger. It can increase a person's heart rate and make them excited.

If you want to draw attention to a design element, use red. But use it as an accent color in moderation as it can be overwhelming.

Orange makes you feel energized and enthusiastic.

Orange enhances a feeling of vitality and happiness. Like red, it draws attention and shows movement but is not as overpowering. It is aggressive but balanced — it portrays energy yet can be inviting and friendly. Orange is great for a call to action to buy or subscribe to a product.

Yellow makes you feel happy and spontaneous.

Yellow is perhaps the most energetic of the warm colors. It is associated with laughter, hope, and sunshine. Accents of yellow help give your design energy and will make the viewer feel optimistic and cheerful. However, yellow tends to reflect more light and can irritate a person's eyes. Too much yellow can be overwhelming and should be used sparingly. In design, it is often used to grab attention in an energetic and comforting way.

Green makes you feel optimistic and refreshed.

Green symbolizes health, new beginnings, and wealth. Green is the easiest on the eyes and should be used to relax and create balance in a design. It is a great color to use if a company wants to depict growth, security, or inspire possibility. Green can also feel calming and relaxing.

Blue makes you feel safe and relaxed.

Blue evokes feelings of calmness and spirituality as well as security and trust. Seeing the color blue causes the body to create chemicals that are calming. It is no surprise that it's the most favored of the colors. Dark blues are great for corporate designs because it helps give a professional feel, but using too much can create a cold, disengaged feeling. Light blues give a more relaxing, friendly feel. Great examples are social sites like Facebook and Twitter who use lighter blues.

Purple makes you feel creative.

Purple is associated with mystery, creativity, royalty, and wealth. Lighter shades of purple are often used to soothe or calm a viewer, hence why it is used in beauty products. Incorporate purple to make a design look more luxurious and wealthier or a lighter purple to show romance and mystery.

Pink makes you feel playful and romantic.

Pink represents femininity and romance, sensitivity, and tenderness. It's inherently sweet, cute, and charming.

Brown makes you feel down to earth.

Brown creates a sense of stability and support. It's warm and friendly, practical and dependable, and can also represent the old fashioned and well established.

Black feels sophisticated, classic, and serious.

Black evokes power, luxury, elegance, but can also mean professionalism, neutrality, and simplicity. It's bold, powerful and is often used to evoke mystery. In certain contexts, and cultures the color black can also refer to mourning or sadness.

White means minimalism and simplicity. Using a lot of white color in design creates a minimalist aesthetic and can result in a simple, fresh, and clean look.

In many cultures, white is used to refer to virginity, purity, and innocence (think bridal gowns and baby clothes). It's also the most neutral color of all.

Gray feels serious and professional.

Gray is a more mature, responsible color. Its positive connotations include formality and dependability, while the negative side can mean being overly conservative, conventional, and lacking in emotion. It's safe and quite subdued, serious, and reserved.

Using this information as the basis of your logo can be incredibly beneficial to the branding of your business; and will help you to convey a clear message to the world.

Try to keep in mind the aesthetics of your logo. I highly recommend using the Fibonacci sequence when calculating the visual elements of your logo.

Objects that fall under individual or group instances of 1, 3, 5, 8, 13, 21 are more appealing to the human eye. This sequence is used in art and design worldwide.

Moving on from logos, next up is your slogan. Not all businesses require a slogan.

This being said, depending on your intended market, this can be beneficial. If you're using a slogan, make sure you keep it simple. No one identifies with a wordy slogan.

The words should also fall under the Fibonacci sequence, I recommend using three words to get your point across; it's short, sweet, and punchy.

Using these elements and visual design mediums such as "Canva", or "Photoshop" will be beneficial in your physical and/or internet presence. You also have the option of outsourcingg the designs. I reccomend platforms like Upwork or Fiverr. You will likely get more bang for your buck, and help someone on their journey.

Your created images will serve as a solid foundation for any social media accounts your business may have. Social media is a great branding tool and can make a massive difference in the reach of your business. I recommend setting up a business email for any social accounts, as this can help your inbox remain focused and spam-free; it will also help with billing and invoicing covered in the next chapter.

CHAPTER 6: INVOICES AND BILLING

You've got a business, a brand, and some method of sales, be it online or a physical location.

One of the biggest hurdles for many startups is invoicing and billing.

It can be a little confusing.

For example, you have managed to start a service business for lawn maintenance.

Invoices are very simple to make, and there are thousands of free templates you can find online or within your chosen word processing software.

Here's a list of what they need:

Your business logo (optional, but recommended).

Your ABN.

The date of service and the date of the invoice.

Product codes/description (if applicable).

Who the invoice is for (client, company, etc.)

Where the invoice is payable to (BSB and account number).

The timeframe the invoice is payable under (This can vary for 24 hours to 30 days depending on the nature of your business).

You should also reference an invoice number; this is important in keeping track of what invoice has been sent and what is still outstanding.

The reference number can also help to keep track of what's been paid as this is commonly the payment reference when the funds are deposited into your bank account. (if you would like this to happen, state it on the invoice).

I highly recommend adding your contact information: Email, phone number, location, etc.

An invoice is a great opportunity to also add some comments like:

"Thank you for choosing our service"

"If you're happy with the service let your friends, family or co-workers know"

These small comments could make a huge difference in the word of mouth advertising.

You can also include some optional terms and conditions on the invoice if you desire.

If your business has suppliers for stock, you will likely also receive an invoice or receipt of sale.

Depending on the service it may be a payable window, make sure that funds are transferred before that date to ensure you don't incur any late payment fees.

Your suppliers are your lifeline, treat them well and they should look after you in the long term.

I highly recommend keeping either physical or digital copies of all invoices; incoming and outgoing. I also strongly suggest you begin keeping your receipts. Get a receipt for everything, you never know what you might be able to claim back on tax;conisdering we pay GST on nearly everything.

These will be vital when the end of the financial year, tax time comes around.

CHAPTER 7: BANKING AND TAX

In Australia, there are a variety of options you can choose when it comes to banking.

I like to do things a little differently. There's nothing worse than having to come up with funds to pay the ATO (Australian taxation office). To mitigate this, I always opt for opening two business accounts. One with a debit card for everyday and online use. The other account exists solely as a tax account. Every time you receive a payment to your business account, depending on your annual turnover, I would recommend taking 10-20% out immediately and putting those funds into the tax account. If you prefer doing your banking at a physical bank branch, just ask the staff to complete this action for you.

In regards to superannuation, you have the option, as a soletrader to pay yourself super. It's not mandatory, but it's at your discretion. If you choose to pay yourself super, I highly reccomend Checking into your super fund and making sure that the company invests your money according to your morals. However, if you have staff memebers it is mandatory to pay their super. At the time of writing this, superannuation is 9.5% on top of wages. Be sure to factor this is when expanding and taking on new staff members.

Now you should have an ample amount of money aside come end of the financial year, should you need to pay a lump sum of tax. If you don't need to pay tax, or you pay less than anticipated, you may have some or all of that money left over. I always recommend investing in a good accountant. A good accountant who cares, will help you get the most out of your financials and be an invaluable asset come tax time. If you have a good understanding of accounting and bookkeeping, so be it.

When tax time comes, spend the extra money and get the tax done professionally, you'll get more bang for your buck having it done for you.

Should you have funds leftover, or you get a tax return, there are a variety of different things with that money. There are some actions you can take that will allow you to use those funds as future taxable purchases or activities. Some other choices may be for your gain, at the end of the day I always recommend reinvesting at least one-third of all funds back into the business, one third for upkeep and overheads, and one third for staff and/or paying yourself.

Here are a few ideas:

Use the money for expanding or improving your business.

Use the funds for advertising or a promotional event.

Purchase additional assets for your business. (e.g. Vehicles or property)

Pay yourself a bonus.

This is where financial education comes into play. Financial education is not something we are typically taught growing up, and we are not taught in school. I would highly recommend reading Robert Kiyosaki's bestseller "Rich dad, poor dad" This was one of the most pivotal points in my financial education and helped me to reevaluate my entire outlook on business and money.

On the android store there exists an app that allows you to access all of his works for free digitally; if you don't want to fork out the money to buy the book. It's one of my favorite books, and I recommend it to people at least once or twice a week.

Learn the real difference between assets and liabilities.

A liability is seen very differently, depending where you sit on the class spectrum.

I see my peers buying new cars, and think "that's not even a depreciating asset, that's a growing liability." A liability is anything that costs you money, and doesn't give you anything back, like a car.

An asset is something that can generate you positive cash flow. Positive cash flow is the mother of wealth. Positive passive cahflow is king. An asset should create you cash flow, if it doesn't, its not an asset, it's a liability.

CHAPTER 8: STRUCTURAL INTEGRITY

You're the boss, the big cheese, head honcho.

It all comes down to you. I want you to take a trip down memory lane. We've all had "that one boss" who was and likely still is an absolute dick. Don't be that person. This is where structural integrity comes into action. There's nothing worse than a boss who wants employees to work for them. A good boss, nay, a good leader will work with and for their staff. What you put into your team/s is what you will get out. Your team isn't your family, families are dysfunctional. Think of your team like an engine, if it doesn't have oil, it won't run smoothly. Your job is to be the mechanic. Not only do you give the engine oil, you check the tyres', the battery, the alternator and the electrics.

Your main role is to make sure everything is in good order and operating at maximum efficiency. Efficiency wavers, but its your job to ensure that everyone on your team is working synergistically. Is a staff member having some personal issues? Talk to them, see if they need a day off; it may seem counter productive, but pay them for that day off. It might cost you $100 but are you spending it, or are you investing it into your team. That small investment might mean that staff members' workplace efficiency rises. That team members' respect for you rises, and so does the respect of the other staff members.

Don't forget to invest in the learning of your team members, hold daily, weekly, fortnightly meetings to discuss the previous day, week, month etc. These meetings will allow you to identify any issues that need to be addressed, and also, as a collective unit. Allow the team to come up with ideas on how to alleviate these hurdles in the future. These meetings should be documented and used as additions to your policies and procedures (if your company has or requires them).

Positive workplace culture is diminishing by the day. No one gives a crap about their employees, its all about the dollar bottom line. That's horse shit and you aren't a good leader if you think that's leadership. Support your team on every level; does this, and they will repay you in spades. One of the greatest leadership qualities is being open to new ideas. Adopt the no door policy, literally take it off the hinges. This will allow the creativity and vision of your team to build in the workplace enviroment; and push your business into it's future potential. You never know, a staff member might have stumbled across a great opportunity for your business but you missed it because you know it all.

Be the leader you wish you had. Become the mentor you always wanted, and let your team know that you're in it together. That my friends, is true leadership and will promote a positive workplace culture.

CHAPTER 9: CONTINGENCIES

Contingencies are the "plan B" for any number of circumstances.

Insurance is always top of the list, especially if you have any sort of physical presence.

As a general rule, I recommend public liability insurance. For anything that involves the public.

This will cover you if someone, for example, "slips on an onion" and tries to sue you.

I recommend you insure every asset you and your business own; it's just a smart move.

Your insurance for example should cover but is not limited to theft, fire, and natural disaster.

This includes a business vehicle and physical location. If you are renting a space speak with your Real estate agent about the terms and conditions within your rental agreement. In some rare instances, the owner of the property may be insured. Be sure to ask what the requirements are by the owner.

Another contingency is to always have a surplus of cash in case something happens.

Life, as we know, has the uncanny ability to throw us curve balls at the worst possible time.

Having enough spare cash for at least 3 -6 months' worth of costs is a wise decision. I would also suggest you maintain enough spare funds to cover any insurance premiums.

CHAPTER 9: AGGRESSIVE EXPANSION

If you're looking to scale up, or expand your business. Congratulations, you're already well on your way to becoming very successful.

This is where you need to sit back and take a moment to fully review your business. I suggest you refer back to your business plan, take note of where you started, where you are, and where you want to go. When I say Aggressive expansion, I don't mean become an absolute unit and spread to every corner immediately. Take it one step at a time, but take each step in a calculated but aggressive manner. If you come across a good opportunity, don't let it slip past you, fight for your next move. You've already shown that you can put in the work, what's a little more? The aim of the game is to work now, so you don't have to work again.

For example, if you have a physical retail outlet, and you've built a solid branding, you have some options for expansion. You can opt for physical expansion, which may entail opening another storefront, this can be cumbersome, costly and time consuming. You'll need to research and find a suitable location, go through the leasing process, outfit the store and stock inventory. These costs are primarily tax deductible, and can help offset your profits from the other store.

Alternatively, you could build, or increase your online presence and sales. Consider affiliate marketing, or using local influencers to promote your products. There is also a third position; find a distributer.

Using a distributers' channels, you can accelerate your production and have your garments or items in multiple different stores for sale. This avenue also allows for you to widen your market reach and increase your brand recognition.

Keep your options open, and make sure every step you take in methodically planned out.

If you impulsively jump into the first thing you come across, you could set yourself up for failure.

That being said, don't over think everything to the point where fear stops you from progressing.

There is an incredibly fine line between genius and insanity.

CHAPTER 10: PROFESSIONAL DEVELOPMENT

This is something that we must continuously work on. Your professional development is crucial to your future in the world of business. For example, if you attend networking events or seminars, you may come across someone that has information or connections that could be useful for the future of your business, or your future endeavors.

Seminars are a great place to learn new skills, and change the way you perceive yourself and your business. Even if you attend these events and only learn one new thing, you're in a better position walking ouy those doors, than when you walked in.

Networking events, usually hosted by your local chamber of commerce, are also a great place to get your brand recognised by other bsuiness professionals and potentially score some collaborative work or new clients.

No one is perfect, if you think you know everything, you don't know shit. Keep learning, keep improving, and keep innovating.

Here's to the crazy ones, the misfits, the rebels, the trouble-makers, the round pegs in the square holes... the ones who see things differently — they're not fond of rules... You can quote them, disagree with them, glorify or vilify them, but the only thing you can't do is ignore them because they change things... they push the human race forward, and while some may see them as the crazy ones, we see genius, because the ones who are crazy enough to think that they can change the world, are the ones who do.

—Steve Jobs, 1997

www.ingramcontent.com/pod-product-compliance
Lightning Source LLC
Chambersburg PA
CBHW070520220526

45467CB00002B/769